Still
I Smile

Still I Smile

A Memoir
Finding Joy Amidst Life's Circumstances

WODLINE HIPPOLYTE

Still I Smile
Finding Joy Amidst Life's Circumstances

Cover design by Cooke Classic Branding & Design
Cover photography by Dexterity Productions

ISBN: 978-1-736 9787-0-2

To contact the author, please visit: www.iamwodline.com

The information in this book is true and complete to
the best of the author's knowledge. Some names and
identifying details have been changed to protect the privacy
of the individuals mentioned herein.

Dedication

This book is dedicated to every person who trusted me enough to share his or her story with me. Your courage gave me the strength to share a few chapters of my life. To my readers, I hope that through my story you will find encouragement to forgive the ones who hurt you, to seek healing when you're in pain, and to trust God to do the impossible in your life.

Author's Note

It wasn't until I reached my mid- to late-twenties that I realized I needed people in my life (as early as my teenage years) who were authentic and transparent. I needed folks with some life experience who were genuine enough to be themselves and courageous enough to share their personal stories without feeling ashamed of their pasts. This intimate memoir gives me the opportunity to be the woman I needed in my life over a decade ago. When I began writing this book, I planned to relate only my road to healing after my divorce, but I continued to feel God leading me to share more. Consequently, this book is now a complete memoir, in which I share my traumatic childhood experiences, my painful divorce, my journey of waiting on God, and the struggles I have experienced because of these trials.

There were countless occasions in which I wanted to give up on finishing this manuscript (not least because of the number of years it took to complete it), but I continued to press forward through the feelings of self-doubt and fear and life's detours that almost deterred me. Between a writing coach, beta readers (people who read and provide feedback on your manuscript), and multiple editors and revisions, I was not sure if my book would ever be completed. I believed that God wanted me to share my story of how He brought me through some of the most difficult seasons of my life, but why was it taking so long for it to be ready for publishing?

I started writing this book in 2016, two years after my divorce. Five years later, I am finally able to share my faith story with you. This writing journey has taught me to trust God's timing. If I had decided to move forward with publishing my manuscript when I wanted to, my story would have been told from a place of hurt and anger. It is now told from a different perspective, that of a healed heart. I can also share what God did in my life as I traversed the long road to healing and restoration.

I have written this book for people who were constantly criticized as adolescents and never affirmed by their parents and who now struggle with their confidence; for people who are afraid to be alone and are contemplating settling for less than what they deserve; for people who have been betrayed by the ones to whom they gave their hearts; and for people whose faith is being challenged because things don't seem to be working out in their favor.

If you have experienced trauma at any time in your life, I hope my story will encourage you to work towards the healing you need to move forward. If you're struggling to forgive someone who deeply hurt you, it is my prayer that you will find the strength to forgive them. When I forgave those who hurt me, a heavy weight was lifted from my shoulders. If you are in a relationship and are unsure if you should move forward due to various red flags, I hope you will seek wise counsel from people you trust to determine if it is something you should walk (or run!) away from or continue to engage in. This is something I wish I had done when I started dating.

Are you waiting for a life-changing opportunity or breakthrough? I have been there. I've learned that the time I spent waiting was never wasted time, and that God's timing is always right. It is my hope that while reading my memoir, you will be encouraged by my story of faith and healing and that you will be reminded that you are not alone.

— Wodline Hippolyte
April 2021

Contents

Chapter 1
A Father's Love

My parents and I are Haitian immigrants who came to the United States in the early 1980s after living for a short period in my birthplace: the beautiful island of St. Maarten. Though my parents rarely speak of their childhoods in Haiti, I do know that their lives were characterized by economic insecurity and that they had few opportunities for advancement or education. Like many Haitian young men at the time, my father went abroad in search of work to help his family, eventually finding employment at a hotel on the island of St. Maarten. On one of his trips back to Haiti to visit family, he met my mother, who later married him and accompanied him to St. Maarten, where I was born. Some time later, my father immigrated to the United States, settling in northern New Jersey. My mother and I followed about a year afterwards. My father is one of the hardest working men I know—nothing but death could keep him from missing a day of work. With less than a high school education, he worked multiple jobs in custodial and maintenance services to provide for our family, which eventually grew to six. Due to my father's hard work and sacrifice, my three siblings and I were able to grow up in the suburbs.

We spent most of our childhoods living in a multi-family home my father purchased in the early 1990s. My family lived on the first floor, another family lived on the second, and my father's cousin lived on the third. Though we had little contact with our extended family in the Caribbean, we periodically recorded greetings in Haitian Creole (or sometimes Crenglish, a combination of Creole and English that's very convenient when you've forgotten a word in one language or the other) on cassette tapes to send to our grandparents.

School aside, my siblings' and my lives centered around the local Haitian Baptist church. We attended worship services on Sunday mornings, youth group on Sunday afternoons, and choir rehearsal on Friday evenings. As Christians and non-Christians alike know all too well, church attendance does not make for perfect people. My mother had been raised in a Christian home and tried to be an example of Christian living for her children. My father, on the other hand, came from a religiously mixed family in which some members (including some of his siblings) were devout Christians and others actively practiced witchcraft. Though he often attended church as part of our family routine and worked hard to provide for us materially, he was also the source of the trauma that caused me to repress many of my childhood memories.

Outer appearances were especially important to my father. Growing up I did not feel beautiful. It's hard to feel beautiful when you are constantly criticized. I was conditioned to feel ugly rather than embrace my flaws. When I chipped my front tooth jumping rope, my father made sure that my dentist fixed it immediately. In less than a week, I left the dentist's office with a repaired tooth. My father was willing to spend thousands of dollars to make sure that my sister and I looked flawless in his eyes, which meant braces to straighten our teeth and products to "improve" our skin. Everything had to look perfect. We could have the ugliest hearts as long as we were physically acceptable in his eyes.

I had braces from eighth grade into the first few years of high school, which did not help with my self-esteem because I was self-conscious about how the metal brackets and wires looked on my misaligned teeth. I even had to wear headgear at night, which at the time, was a stereotype used by young actors who portrayed "nerds" on television. I also did not feel beautiful enough to wear clothing that was flattering to my figure, so I wore baggy clothes to hide my body. I preferred wearing men's clothing to dresses, even shopping in the men's department for shirts. I had to wear dresses and skirts to church, but it was back to baggy clothes during the week.

My father was also verbally abusive. The words that came out of his mouth broke me. My father was never proud of me. To be fair, I was not the perfect daughter. Still, he said things no parent should ever say to their child. When he should have spoken life over me, he spoke nothing but death. I made many mistakes growing up and my father brought them up constantly. He always told me of the things

I could not accomplish because of the mistakes I had made. "You will never be nothing," he told me again and again. I will never forget that statement. His words affected the way I saw myself, so much so that it was a constant struggle for me to accept compliments. *You have beautiful eyes. You have a beautiful voice. Great job, Wodline!* Self-doubt would creep in and I would respond simply with a thank you and an awkward smile.

My father rarely spoke about his mother and father, but from what I have been told, he and his siblings were raised in a verbally and physically abusive household. It is my understanding that his parents enjoyed abusing their children. When I learned this, I did not know how to respond. How can parents cause such harm to their children? My father had had a traumatic upbringing, and unfortunately, he repeated the same cycle with his own family.

His form of discipline traumatized me. In addition to the first floor of our house, my family also had sole access to an unfinished basement, which we used for storage and as a laundry room. This was the place where my father would take me to be disciplined. Anytime I was sent to the basement, I knew it was not going to be a good night.

Like most adolescents, there were days when I was disobedient, dishonest, and misbehaved. My father was the one who did most of the disciplining. If his mission was to instill fear, he succeeded. "Excessive physical discipline" would be an understatement. He used a switch, an extension cord, and a rod that we had from a broken tent, called "Charlie," to discipline me.

Once, a visiting pastor at my church, who was very prideful about how he was raising his children, gave a sermon in which he boasted about "Charlie," something he used to discipline his children. Out of everything my father heard that morning, his takeaway was "Charlie." My father seemed a little too excited to have his own "Charlie" with which to discipline us. He left the rod at the top of our bedroom door frame as a constant reminder of what misbehavior would bring. I hated "Charlie." "Go get Charlie," was my least favorite statement that came out of my father's mouth. Who names the thing with which they discipline their child? Anytime I saw that pastor out in the community or at my church, I was reminded of why my father disciplined me with a tent rod called "Charlie" and of the trauma I suffered at home.

As a preteen, I made one of the worst decisions of my life: I stole money from one of my parents' closest friends. When my parents found out, they were so disappointed in me. It was a night I will never forget. I was taken to the basement, where my father tied up my wrists and my feet with a telephone cord. I had to lie on my stomach on the cold basement floor. He covered my mouth with duct tape and beat me with either an extension or telephone cord. As he beat me, I could hear my mother helplessly screaming behind the locked basement door for him to stop. I heard her say that she was going to get help from my dad's cousin who lived on the third floor. With the door locked and an immigrant mom who was probably afraid to get the police involved, no one ever came to my rescue.

With everything I faced at home, I became an angry young woman. On the outside, I was mean, but on the inside, I was broken, waiting for someone to rescue me. I was dying inside and thought no one could save me. No one knew what was going on at home. I was not the nicest person to my friends at church, especially my male friends.

I needed to stop believing the lies my father told me and to see myself the way God saw me and to find security in my identity as His child.

I did not know how to cope with the pain I was experiencing internally, so I hurt people both verbally and physically. One boy from church used to call me Wolverine because I took pleasure in digging my nails into his arm with the intent to cause pain. I hurt people before I allowed them to hurt me.

How was my father supposed to show me what love was when he did not know what it looked like? How was he supposed to give love if his parents had never given it to him? Did he not love himself or our family enough to try to break this cycle? Did he not see how his behavior was emotionally unhealthy? Why would he put his children through the same thing he experienced as a child? Why didn't he pray for God to heal those broken places in his life? Did he want to be healed? Did he want to be delivered? Did he love himself? Did he love my mother? Did he think that marrying my mother would heal his brokenness?

These were questions I constantly asked myself. My father loved me the only way he knew how – by being a provider – but I needed more than that. In hindsight, I needed to stop believing the lies my father told me and to see myself the way God saw me and to find security in my identity as His child. As an angry and broken teenager, however, that was a lesson I was not yet prepared to learn. Instead, since I did not love myself, I went looking for someone to love me, to make me feel beautiful. Toward the end of my junior year of high school, I found that someone ... or so I thought.

Chapter 2

My First Love

During the spring of my junior year of high school, I started a relationship with Jason, a young man I knew from both my childhood and church. When we were younger, we lived across the street from each other until he and his family moved to the next town over. Over the years, Jason and his family frequented and eventually became members of the church my family attended. Jason was involved in the same ministry in which I served. Since he was one year younger than I am, the thought of us being a couple never crossed my mind. However, the more I saw him in church, the more I became attracted to his charming personality.

Our romantic relationship was something I did not expect. It happened one evening after a dance ministry concert. One of Jason's friends handed me a note from him asking me to be his girlfriend. I said yes—it was one of the happiest moments of my teenage life! Someone actually found me worthy enough to want me as his girlfriend.

Jason was my first boyfriend, my first kiss, and the first guy to whom I said, "I love you." It felt so good to have someone in my life who accepted me with all my flaws! I was on cloud nine. Though his family and my friends knew from the beginning, I initially tried to keep our relationship a secret from my family. Once my parents found out, my father was not pleased. I received a long lecture from him about why I should not have a boyfriend and why Jason was not good for me. (For example, he was not "a typical church boy.") I cried in our living room throughout the lecture because my father was trying to take from me the one thing that made me happy. He refused to accept our relationship, but later relented when he realized I was not going to let go of the "man" who made me feel beautiful.v

During the honeymoon stages of our relationship, I felt as if I was on top of the world. I had never felt so beautiful and wanted. Jason always affirmed me and made me feel special. For example, on Valentine's Day during my senior year of high school, I was called down to the office. I was a little nervous. *Why would I be called to the school office?* I was a good student and never got into any trouble. When I reached the office, some Valentine's Day balloons and a beautifully packaged rose were waiting for me. Jason had had them delivered to the school. That made my day! Sadly, because our relationship was still a secret to my parents at the time, there was no way I could take home those wonderful balloons. One of my friends graciously took them, while I kept the rose. I was now lying to my parents and involving my friend in that lie. (The fact that I had to hide this relationship was a clear sign that I should not have entered it, though I couldn't see that at the time.) I did not want to lose Jason, so I continued to live this lie until my mother found out and told my father.

Once my family and our church knew that Jason and I were a couple, I felt as if a load had been lifted from me. Nevertheless, there were quite a few people who were surprised that I chose to date this boy since I was a ministry leader. In my church, there was an unspoken rule that young men or women in leadership would date and eventually marry someone who was also a leader. Some thought I should date someone who was on the path to becoming a pastor. One Sunday after the morning service, I was cornered by a church member who boldly said in Haitian Creole, "I'm giving you one year," referring to my relationship, which he believed would not last. I just smiled and went about my business. My uncle (who was very judgmental, so I did not want him to know about my relationship with Jason) went even further, telling me that my boyfriend would never be ready for marriage and that I was wasting my time. I did not have much to say in response to him, either. I thanked him and went back to whatever I was doing. What did he know about my boyfriend and our relationship?

Unfortunately, I wanted our relationship to work so badly that I fell in love with Jason's potential and not who he truly was. I wanted to prove everyone wrong. Throughout our relationship, we talked about marriage. I even checked out wedding dresses online a few times. I was so young and naïve. Jason talked about how he was considering becoming a pastor and how he would be different from the ones we knew. We had both witnessed hypocrisy from church leaders and Jason promised that he would not be like them. This gave me hope that he could be the man I desired him to be spiritually, a man who could lead his family in the way the Bible called husbands to lead. When you want something badly enough, you begin to believe the lies you tell yourself. That was me. Deep down inside, I knew Jason was not the man God had for me, but I was so "in love" that I wanted him to be my first and only love.

While we never had sex with one another, I was playing with fire. During our relationship, I put myself in compromising situations that went against everything I was taught. I awakened desires that should have been saved for my future spouse. I will not pretend that I never thought about taking that next step with him. When we passionately kissed, I found myself desiring more. The temptation to have sex with the person whom I was in love with was real. I knew better but convinced myself that as long as we were not having sex, we were good.

As our relationship progressed, the temptation to have sex grew stronger, but I still held out. I knew he wanted to. He referred to the act as "making love" and not just "having sex." He never pressured me, but he said all the right things to make me question whether I should just go ahead and do it. When he realized that I was not going to sleep with him, he became frustrated. I remember one day we had a phone conversation that left me hurt. With somewhat of an attitude, he called me a prude. It felt as if he had ripped my heart out and stomped on it. That was one of the first times he had said something that hurt me. However, even though it hurt, I did not allow his insult to change my mind about having sex before marriage.

Not only was I faced with temptation, but this relationship was also a distraction during my first two years of college. Between being a student, serving in church ministry, and living in an emotionally unhealthy home, spending time with Jason was my escape from reality. He helped me forget what I was dealing with at home, so much so that I made our relationship a priority instead of my education. From leaving my classes early to spend time with him to not giving school and church work my best effort, I allowed my need to be loved to come before everything else. Nevertheless, it was also during this time that we began to drift apart.

Breaking up with my first love was one of the hardest decisions I had to make in my early twenties. We were at a place where we both knew it was not going to work; he was going in one direction and I in another. I was trying to grow deeper in my faith, but he was not interested in doing the same. We broke up on a Friday. In church two days later, the youth choir (of which I was a part) had to sit in the choir seats on the platform facing the congregation for the entire service. It was not easy for me to have to look at some of the faces of the people in the congregation, especially those who had had something to say about my relationship with Jason. That one member had been right: we did not last long. It was hard to get through that service without crying. After it was over, I found myself in one of the side rooms of the altar crying as I told our choir director that my boyfriend and

I had broken up. She comforted me and assured me that I would be okay. Even though Jason and I had ended things on good terms, I was still heartbroken.

One of the biggest mistakes I made after we broke up was operating as if we were still in a relationship. How did I expect to move on and heal if I was still kissing him? I was not thinking about the other young women he could have been entertaining. I was not thinking about how hurt I would be if I found out that he had moved on. I learned the hard way why we should have remained friends and nothing more. One morning, my friend called me to share what Jason had been telling people about our relationship. He had told his friends we had done some sexual things, things that had never actually happened. This caused unnecessary drama between both groups of friends. There was a lot of "he said, she said" and friends taking sides. Though I knew the truth, I got tired of trying to defend myself. I was angry, hurt, and ashamed. I felt I had let God and the young people I was serving down. I consequently emailed an apology to the youth of the ministry I served for not being the woman of God I had portrayed myself to be. Thankfully, I was able to continue as their leader. It was a humbling experience because I had been judgmental towards many young people during that season of my life. I learned that just because someone's sins were different from mine

> *I learned that just because someone's sins were different from mine didn't mean that I was any better than they were.*

didn't mean that I was any better than they were. After all the drama between Jason and me settled down, we were able to be cordial with one another, leaving what had happened in the past. After that, I remained single for a little over a year before I entered my next relationship.

Chapter 3

A Match Made in Heaven

About a year-and-a-half after breaking up with Jason, I was introduced to a young man named François at a Labor Day block party hosted by the youth ministry of a local church in Orange, New Jersey. A young lady from the youth ministry I was leading at the time knew him from high school. She suggested that he play the piano at our upcoming talent show, so she gave me his phone number to further discuss the opportunity, to which he later agreed. During the show, François caught my attention as he played the hymn, "I Surrender All" on the keyboard. Though I was accustomed to singing and listening to hymns in church, I'd never heard one played as smoothly, beautifully, and confidently as François's solo that night. We talked more after the show and soon became friends.

At first, our relationship was strictly platonic. I was not looking for romance and he was going through a rough patch with his girlfriend. Nevertheless, we spoke to each other more frequently than I expected. I was there for moral support, encouraging him as he tried to figure out his relationship. His girlfriend's name was very similar to mine, and he would accidentally call me by her name from time to time. Isn't that crazy?!

As our friendship progressed, I began to develop feelings for him. I was not sure what those feelings were until I took a trip to Florida with my mother. Before I left, he told me to call him when I got back. In my mind, I thought that meant not to contact him until I got back. While I was away, I could not stop thinking about him and wanted to reach out to him. When I returned to New Jersey, I told him about the trip. I told him about how I had wanted to call him but had decided not to because of what he had said. We both laughed about how I had taken his words so literally. As the days went on, I finally found the courage to tell him about my feelings for him. To my relief, he felt the same way. We became an official couple a few weeks later.

Unlike with Jason, I did not feel the need to hide my relationship with François. We knew several of the same people because of our involvement in the Haitian church community. As the months passed by, we met each other's friends, families, and church families. I met his family and church family on the same day. My mother made sure I wore my Sunday best – an ivory dress – that day so that I would look beautiful from head to toe. Even though I thought I looked cute, I was so nervous. François picked me up that morning to attend Sunday school followed by Sunday service. He was the church's keyboardist, so I had to sit alone in the left front pew while he was playing. It was a nerve-racking experience to say the least! I met his family after the service. Though his mother had a few concerns about me, his father welcomed me warmly.

My parents, on the other hand, had the exact opposite reactions. My mother welcomed François with open arms, but my father had a few reservations about him. He was concerned that François was an entrepreneur who had been between jobs when we started dating. I think he would have preferred that my boyfriend have a steady, nine-to-five job that would support a family should we decide to get married. I, however, was young, still in college, and in love—those kinds of concerns weren't a part of my life yet.

François was different than Jason. He prayed with me over the phone at night, which was something I was not used to. I loved his enthusiasm for music and his heart to serve the young people in his church. François and I founded a ministry together during the early stages of our relationship, PS 150:6 Ministries (later called Perfect Harmony Ministries). I grew up in a Haitian Baptist church where many of the young people were denied the opportunity to attend their high schools' proms because their parents felt that proms were too worldly. This ministry was birthed with these young folks in mind. François supported my vision wholeheartedly, which made me love him even more. Our first event was an *Evening of Elegance* where youth and young adults were invited to wear formal attire and enjoy an evening of food, fellowship, and dancing. The event was booked to take place in June, nine months after François and I had started dating.

Several weeks before the event, as one of my girlfriends and I shopped in K&G Fashion Superstore, we were approached by an older gentleman who began questioning us about our boyfriends. He somehow knew that our boyfriends were both musicians and shared things only someone who knew them would know. He told us that we should leave them because they were not good for us. My girlfriend just laughed it off. I, on the other hand, ended my relationship with François. My friend and her boyfriend thought I was foolish to break up with him due to a conversation with a stranger in a clothing store. However, I did not believe it was a coincidence that we were approached by that gentleman. I honestly thought that the man was being used by God. How else could he have known so much about François? Even though I was the one who ended our relationship, we both were hurt by my decision. And even though we were both hurt, we still had an event to host. The venue and vendors were booked. Tickets were already sold. We could not cancel this highly-anticipated event. It was awkward, but we managed to get through it.

Then began an emotionally tough summer. There was a lot of back-and-forth drama between François's friends and mine. His friends felt that it had been unwise of me to have broken up with someone they considered to be a good man. People's many opinions only added more stress to an already confusing situation. My only reason to break up with François was that a stranger had told me that he was not good for me. Part of me questioned if I had indeed made the right decision in ending our relationship.

A few weeks after an *Evening of Elegance*, I found myself at my former boyfriend Jason's family barbeque on the Fourth of July. It was a bit awkward being there, but one of my girlfriends had encouraged me to get out of the house and attend. What made things even more uncomfortable was seeing Jason with his new girlfriend. I had to pretend that seeing them together did not bother me. As I sat on the front steps of the house, one of his friends tried to comfort and encourage me. He had heard about my recent breakup and told me that I would be okay. At that moment, I wanted to break down and cry. I may not have said a lot, but my facial expressions said everything: I was not okay; I was hurt.

Seeing that I was overwhelmed with uncertainty, my mom helped me book a trip to Florida to spend a week with one of my cousins, Denise, to clear my head. I needed to get away from everything and everyone in New Jersey. Though Denise is older, we are close enough in age to be able to relate to one another on many issues. We were able to have honest, transparent conversations because she kept it real with me, which I loved (and still love!) about her. To be able to have someone to talk to who was not a part of the drama and confusion at home allowed me to see things from a different perspective. Denise went the extra mile to make sure I had the perfect experience in Florida. One of the highlights of the trip was going to my first movie at a drive-in theater. Her intention was to help me forget about what had happened in New Jersey, and she did an excellent job. I did not want the trip to end, but I had to get back to the reality of finding a resolution to my breakup with François. Would we reconcile as a couple or go our separate ways?

François also left New Jersey at about the same time I did and traveled to Georgia with some friends to attend MegaFest, one of the largest Christian events in the country. While there, they stayed with family members of one of his friends. François quickly became acquainted with this friend's female cousin. Soon, another one of his friends on the trip began to taunt me that I was about to lose my ex-boyfriend to another woman. The news hurt me, but I wasn't sure if I had a right to be mad. I was the one who had broken up with him after all.

Despite a summer full of drama and uncertainty, we reunited as a couple that fall. François was my best friend and confidant. We shared a love for music and the arts. We were there for one another when we had separate ministry engagements. We supported each other's career goals. François knew everything about me. He treated me well. He cooked for me. He picked me up after class and helped me with some of my coursework. He gave me the emotional support I needed, especially when things were not going well at home with my father.

As our relationship progressed, I saw a future with François. We began spending more time with one another and with each other's families. When possible, we visited each other's churches for special events. Though no relationship is perfect, I overlooked potential red flags when friends vaguely expressed their disapproval of François. Several people commented about his questionable business practices, while another young adult strongly stressed the need for us to go through pre-marital counseling (which we had been planning to do anyway). François, however, had answers for everything, which I accepted without much question. I loved François and wanted our relationship to work. I did not want to be judgmental towards him or his past but wanted to show him the same grace that God continued to show me.

François and I were married on a beautiful fall day in late September, approximately two years after we reconciled as a couple, with about two hundred of our friends and family in attendance. I felt beautiful in my bright white wedding gown, which I was so excited to wear. White is meant to symbolize purity, and François and I had resisted the temptation to consummate our relationship before our wedding.

While reading a dating devotional some time later, however, I came across the following scripture verse from one of Paul's letters: "Having lost all sense of shame, they have given themselves over to sensuality for the practice of every kind of impurity, with a craving for more" (Eph. 4:19, BSB). It dawned on me that purity was not limited to sexual intercourse, and that I had not been worthy of the color of my wedding dress. Growing up in church, sex was not discussed in detail, though we were given plentiful scripture references to reinforce the belief that premarital sex was a sin. Wearing a white bridal gown was something I had originally felt so proud about. In my eyes, I was pure because I had not engaged in sexual intercourse. Nevertheless, François and I had not set healthy boundaries for ourselves when it came to where and how we physically expressed our love for each other. In moments of passionately making out with each other, we had abandoned ourselves to doing things that seemed "okay" because we were not having sex, but that were still impure in God's eyes. Though we were both serving in young adult ministries, we were not walking the walk. I am forever grateful that God showed us mercy by not exposing us.

Hindsight aside, our wedding day was everything I had envisioned it would be. Our theme was *A Match Made in Heaven*. Gold and white were incorporated into everything. My bridesmaids wore gold satin dresses accented with a white belt and pickups in the skirt to complement my wedding gown. François and his groomsmen wore full-length white mandarin collar tuxedos with gold vests to complement the bridesmaids' gowns. Our ceremony was held at his church, which was decorated with white drapes at the entrance, down the pews, and at the altar. We had a live band and a performance by the praise dance ministry from my church. As my father walked me down the aisle to a live performance of Maurette Brown Clark's "The One He Kept for Me," I heard my cousin, who I had not seen in a few years, whisper, "Smile!" At that moment, I smiled, but I was nervous because I hated being the center of attention. Once we reached the end of the aisle, my father gave me away and handed me over to my fiancé. François and I exchanged traditional wedding vows and rings and lit the unity candle. After we were pronounced husband and wife, we walked down the aisle and exited the sanctuary with our wedding party and parents. Our attendants remained at the church with us to take a few post-ceremony photos before we headed to the reception venue.

François and I arrived at the venue in a white Rolls Royce. As we entered the building, I was excited to enjoy the cocktail hour and dinner reception with our friends and family. The main ballroom complemented our wedding colors with its gold and white walls. The amber-lit ballroom was filled with floating candles and red rose petals. It was a heartwarming experience to be surrounded by loved ones who had traveled from near and far to celebrate our union. That night I had the most fun I had had in a long time. After the reception was over, we said farewell to our guests and headed to our hotel.

The next morning, we overslept and missed our flight for our honeymoon! We were able to book new flights and were off the next day to the stunning island of Maui in Hawaii. François had rented a beautiful home with a gorgeous view of the rainforest. It rained almost every day we were there, but that did not keep us from enjoying the honeymoon experience. We cooked together, went to a luau, and had a masseuse come over to pamper us. If this was what our marriage was going to look like, I was very excited about what was in store for the coming years.

Chapter 4

Shattered Dreams

Unlike our honeymoon in Maui, our marriage was not perfect. We went through many tests and trials over the following years. Some of these struggles were typical of married couples: navigating the merger of two different lives, dealing with job loss, and handling financial difficulties. However, some of our trials were unsettling, such as François's lack of honesty regarding money. Not long into our marriage, I discovered that he had lied about how much he made. I never confronted him about it, but my trust in him started to deteriorate as a result.

Still, by God's grace, we were able to overcome our troubles and decided that we wanted to start a family. We conceived our first child, a son, months after trying to get pregnant. Our son was born via an emergency C-section – somehow the umbilical cord was wrapped around his arm – three years and a day after our wedding date. Thankfully, there were no health complications, and we were able to take our baby home from the hospital a couple of days later.

Two years after our son was born, we celebrated our fifth wedding anniversary with a dinner at a catering venue for about 60 of our closest friends and family. This meant a lot to me because I knew of many young couples who had not made it to their fifth year of marriage. Part of what made the day so special was that our white stretch SUV limo was from the same company where we had rented our car for our wedding day. I designed all the stationery for the party, including the invitations, menus, table numbers, and seating chart, as well as the floral centerpieces. I felt like a queen that day in my strapless satin champagne evening gown with pickups in the skirt, just like the dresses my bridesmaids had worn on our wedding day. François and our son wore matching black pants and white tuxedo jackets. We hired my friend who was a professional photographer to capture our intimate affair and one of my favorite deejays to keep our guests entertained. The evening was filled with great food, music, dancing, and catching up with friends we had not seen in a while. When the deejay played the song "African Queen" by 2Face Idibia, François swept me onto the dance floor. As we danced, he sang the words to me and my heart melted. I did not have a care in the world. I was in the arms of the man I loved surrounded by our loved ones. It was an evening to remember.

Two months later, Thanksgiving arrived. François, our son, and I had an early dinner with my family. After dinner, François stepped out to meet with a client because he said he had something the client needed from him. Since he worked in the tax accounting industry, it was not unusual for a client to ask him for documents, but this time I did not believe him. It was not tax season, and I thought the last thing anyone would want to do on Thanksgiving Day was to work. I couldn't shake the feeling that something was not right, but I let it go because I was afraid to face the possibility that he might have a mistress.

A couple of days later, while I was on François's iPad, I found photos of a young woman dressed in a sexy outfit sitting down in what looked like a club. When I questioned him about it, he assured me that she was "just a friend," but that did not sit well with me. Why would a married man have photos of a woman who is not his wife or family member on his iPad, especially one dressed the way she was? I wanted to believe him, but deep down inside I knew he was lying.

The next day, I confronted him about the photos via text message while he was at work. I began sending him back-to-back texts trying to find out who the mystery woman was. I started the thread with, "I hope she's worth it." I was certain that he was hiding something from me and felt an urgent need to discover the truth. I went looking for a fight, not knowing I was going to lose. "Really?" he responded. His subsequent replies made it clear that it was not the time to have this conversation because he was working. I had not thought about who he was working with at the time or how my texts might have added stress to his workday. Once I realized that my efforts were not getting me anywhere or helping the situation, I let it go for the day. Part of me felt silly because I could have waited until he got home to have had the conversation.

From that "conversation" on, my behavior toward him changed. There were a couple of nights I did not sleep in our bedroom. I probably should have sent him to sleep on the couch in the living room, but I chose to sleep on the futon across the hallway in our home office. How could I sleep next to someone who could be having an affair? I did not know how to process what I was going through. Nevertheless, one night, even with all the tension between us, I found it in me to have dinner waiting for him when he got home from work. Growing up, that is what I saw my mother do with my father. No matter how dysfunctional things were at home, my mother always had a meal waiting for him. I now know that was an unhealthy dynamic that allowed the dysfunction to continue because it did not create change towards a healthier marriage.

The following Wednesday, I was sitting on the couch in our dimly lit living room as François got settled in from work. He came into the living room to speak with me. As he stood in front of me, I no longer recognized him as he stared at me with a discontented expression. We talked about the tension we had been experiencing over the past few days. After a brief conversation, he announced that he felt that he should spend a few days at his father's house. He grabbed a few of his belongings and left the apartment. I was paralyzed, and remained on the couch feeling hurt, confused, and angry.

After François left, I spent lonely nights crying myself to sleep. I went days without eating. I did not tell anyone what was going on in my life. His father and two brothers were the only ones who knew he was not at home because he was living with them. Nevertheless, my father-in-law was our biggest cheerleader. He called and texted me encouraging words about how he was praying for us. He wanted our marriage to work as much as I did. He told me not to worry, and that his son would be back home in no time.

About a week after François left, our son was set to perform at a Christmas concert hosted by his preschool. Both of our families were planning to go, so I begged François to attend the event as a couple because I was ashamed to let my family know that he had left me. He reluctantly agreed, and we sat together in the church where the concert was held. (My father-in-law was convinced that this would prompt François to return home.) Throughout the concert, I acted like nothing was wrong. It was hard to keep it together. I missed my best friend and wanted him back home. As he sat towards the end of the pew, with me to his right, I tried to engage in a conversation with him, but he seemed uninterested in speaking to me. I tried sitting closer to him, but he moved over. He was avoiding me while he sat right next to me. I felt rejected. When the concert was over, François dropped off my son and me at home and promptly left. Entering the apartment, I felt hopeless because it did not look like François would ever return home.

One evening, I called one of my closest friends, Gabrielle, to tell her about François and me. She dropped everything to come over to my apartment. I was an emotional mess that evening. As I shared with her what was going on, I had to relive everything that had happened. The situation did not make any sense to her because she had just seen us together at our son's school event. She had also been at our fifth wedding anniversary celebration three months earlier. She had thought we were doing well. That made me feel even worse.

While Gabrielle was there, I reached out to my mentor from church. I could barely get through our conversation because I was crying hysterically. My mentor recommended that I call the church to seek counseling and ended our phone conversation with a prayer. I was in the most vulnerable season of my life. It was hard to share what was going on, but my marriage was in trouble and we needed outside intervention.

When I finally told my family that François and I had separated, they were hurt but not surprised. My mother had sensed that something was wrong but had been waiting for me to say something. She knew me well enough to know that I was not the kind of person to spontaneously share all the things going on in my life. My siblings admitted that they felt François was not a man of integrity because of things they had picked up on during their interactions with him. My mother, however, took our separation hard. She had loved and trusted François as her son. It seemed that it took her longer than me to come to terms with his actions.

One afternoon, I went to see my mom. I just sat in the kitchen while she tended to her chores. I was brokenhearted and voiced my concern about how I was going to take care of myself and my son. I was a stay-at-home mom in the early stages of growing a business. In her tough mom's voice, she assured me that I was going to be okay. My family would be there for me and I had nothing to worry about because of God's faithfulness. Then, out of nowhere, she commented, "At least you're not pregnant." I again broke down as the tears spilled down my cheeks. I had taken a home pregnancy test just the week before that had come back positive.

I was desperate to have my pregnancy confirmed by a doctor, but it was too early to be seen by my OB/GYN. I did not have health insurance, so I decided to visit a health clinic in town. As I nervously walked into the building and greeted the front desk receptionist, I was told that they were unable to help me that day and that I would have to come back at another time. I decided to visit another clinic that was about fifteen minutes from my apartment. When I arrived, the waiting room was full of people. I signed in and took a seat. The wait was longer than I had expected. I became impatient and went to the front desk to ask how much longer I would have to wait to be seen. When the receptionist could not give me a definitive answer, I decided to leave. As soon as I got into my car, I began to weep. I felt helpless. I did not know where to go or what to do. I went home defeated and decided to wait until I was further along to be seen by my OB/GYN.

When I finally decided to tell François about the positive pregnancy test, he was not pleased. The fact that I told him I was not going to tell him anything about it did not help the situation. I wasn't going to tell him because I wasn't sure if being pregnant would help or hurt our situation. I think deep down I wanted him to return home because he wanted to and not because he had a child on the way. "I stayed for the kids." I didn't want that to be my story.

Regardless of what he thought, if it was a viable pregnancy, I already knew that I was not going to terminate it. This made me even more anxious to see a doctor. How was I going to raise two kids when my marriage was in trouble. Weeks later, I had an early miscarriage. My mom walked with me every step of the way as I tried to heal from yet another loss.

That Christmas, all I wanted was François back home. I thought it was my behavior over the photos that had pushed him away, so one day I asked him, "How do I make things right? When will you come back home?" The conversation did not go as expected. François told me he had one foot out the door and one foot in. Then I did something I thought I would never do: as I sat on the couch in our living room, I desperately begged my husband to come back home while he stood near the apartment door ready to leave. He looked at me as if there was nothing I could do or say that would change his mind. (Looking back, I cannot believe I did that. My advice? Never beg anyone to stay in a relationship with you. If someone wants to go, sometimes you must let them.) I was devastated. My husband did not know if he wanted to come back or not. Was I not worth coming back to? I knew that I had made some mistakes, but I did not think the tension we experienced around Thanksgiving was reason enough for either of us to walk away from our marriage.

It was hard to stay encouraged because François's actions continued to show me that he did not want to return. He would come by the apartment to pick up his clothing and belongings little by little. Seeing him come back and forth to pick up his things was torture. Every time he walked through our apartment door, I thought he was coming back home to stay, but he never did. I did not understand why he would not return. We had had fights and disagreements before. There had to be more to him leaving than what he was telling me … so I decided to sign in to both his personal and business email accounts.

What I found deeply hurt me because the man I had trusted with my heart had been lying to me. The young woman who was "just a friend" was more than a friend. She was saved as "Queen" in his contacts. (What married man saves a friend in his contacts as "Queen"?!) Over the next few weeks, I began compiling "proof" of his extramarital relationship through email conversations, bank statements, phone records, and photos. I found pictures of them together and of her alone. Searching through his email became a daily routine – it was like an addiction. The more I went searching for proof, the more I hurt myself. I even found things involving other women, including one I had met before. I do not know if they had a sexual relationship, but she was comfortable enough to send him pictures of herself in lingerie.

Could this be the reason why François had talked about canceling our anniversary celebration several months ago? Maybe it was because he knew there was nothing to celebrate. Any time I reminisced about that evening, I wondered about a few men who were close to François who had not attended the party. My husband had told me that these men were coming with their wives or significant others, yet they never showed up.

. . .I realize that instead of using all my time and energy to compile proof of his extramarital relationship, I should have been seeking counsel. I should have been praying.

Perhaps they knew the truth about where my husband stood with our marriage and did not want to cosign on a lie. Why celebrate with a man who was living a double life? Or maybe François had never bothered to send them the invitations to deny them the opportunity to warn me about his infidelity.

François had betrayed me. He had hurt me. I was ashamed. I was embarrassed. I felt so stupid. I felt ugly. I felt unworthy. I felt dirty. Yet I knew that I did not deserve to be treated this way. The more I continued to do my investigative work, the more broken I became. I began comparing myself to the other woman. She was ten years younger than I which made me feel less confident about myself. I felt like I was living in a Lifetime movie in which the husband leaves his wife for a younger woman. I could not believe this was happening to me. Was my husband going to destroy our marriage over this girl?

In hindsight, I realize that instead of using all my time and energy to compile proof of his extramarital relationship, I should have been seeking counsel. I should have been praying. After the new year began, I finally decided to let him know that I had gone into his email accounts. I printed out the things I had on him, as well as a typed nine-page letter expressing how this whole situation made me feel. I gave it all to him when he dropped off our son after preschool. I could tell by the look on his face that he did not know what to expect in the envelope. Maybe he thought they were divorce papers. He smirked and took the envelope. Several hours later, I checked to see if he had changed his email passwords ... and he had! He was livid.

Days after he received the packet, I suggested that we go to counseling. He was not interested, but I still decided to call the church. It was one of the most awkward conversations I have ever had with someone in church leadership. I was asked specific questions as to why we were separated and about the infidelity. I was embarrassed. The church got back to me a few days later with possible dates for us to come in. François reluctantly agreed to attend the session and I confirmed our chosen date with the church.

We were set to meet on a Monday afternoon towards the end of January. I almost got into a car accident with someone who ran a stop sign, as I anxiously drove to the session. I was shaken by the experience, but I was determined to get to the church for counseling. When François arrived, it was clear he did not want to be there. He came dressed in a suit which I thought was a bit much, especially because I had worn jeans and a blouse. His attitude and attire showed that he had somewhere more important to be. During the session, we both had the opportunity to express our feelings. When he spoke, it seemed to be coming from a place of hurt and anger. He tried to justify his behavior and relationship with the other woman. When it was my turn, I cried through most of everything I had to share. François seemed unfazed by my tears. The counselors recommended that we read *His Needs, Her Needs* by Willard F. Harley Jr. At the end of the session, they had us hold hands as they prayed for us. I left feeling hurt and disappointed. How could anyone put the person they claimed to love through this? It was the first and last marital counseling session we would ever have.

After I got home from the session, I immediately ordered the recommended book. Once it arrived, I completed it in a week. At first, I was upset after reading the book. It forced me to recognize the mistakes I had made during our five years of marriage. I had put career pursuits, ministry, and being a mother before my husband. He had not been one of my top priorities. I had not met his needs as my husband. Our marriage was not affair-proof and we both played a role in that, even though he had been the one to break our vows and to leave.

For a while, then, I believed that I was the reason my marriage was in shambles, but the more I learned about François and his past, the more I realized that our marriage had been in trouble long before it even began. Our marriage had been built on a foundation of lies. François had told me many half-truths and had omitted many stories of his past. I now understood why, during our counseling session, one of the counselors said that we needed to break the foundation on which our marriage was built and construct a new one.

Over the next few months, I found myself pouring my heart out to anyone who would listen, from my family to his family and from my friends to his friends (who had become my friends). That is when I learned that I had to watch who I spoke to. Though I had trusted them, François's family repeated to him the things I had shared with them. (I guess I should not have been surprised. He was their son. He was their brother.) Everyone had an opinion about our separation and had advice they wanted to give me. Talking to too many people caused much confusion in my life. I had so many people in my ear that I could not hear the voice of God.

There were times when I felt that I was being pressured to make an immediate decision about my marriage. Should I stay and fight? This meant fervently praying that François would be opened to consistently go to marriage counseling to help resolve our problems. Should I give up and walk away? I wasn't sure if I could ever trust him again. I was torn and confused. I needed to tune out the voices of family and friends in order to tune in to God's voice.

As I shared my heart with people, one thing I began to find out was how they truly felt about François. People now told me they thought I could have done better. Some expressed that he was not good enough for me and that he could not be trusted. And yet these folks had never attempted to warn me *before* our wedding. They had felt that it was not their place to say anything and reasoned that I was so in love that I would not have listened anyway. I could not help wondering, *Why did you come to our wedding? Why did we spend all that money for you to have a good time at our reception if you never supported our relationship?* There was a part of me that was initially hurt by this, but after people explained their reasons for keeping quiet, I understood.

Not only did our separation affect me but it affected our son as well. For weeks, he would wake up in the middle of the night around the same time crying out for me. He would turn on all the lights in our apartment. He would say things like, "Mommy, I could not find you" or "Mommy, I thought you were gone." It broke my heart. I constantly had to reassure him that I was still there and that I was not going anywhere. I did not know if his behavior was caused by his father no longer living with us or if he kept having the same nightmare. (A pastor friend told me that François leaving the family home was likely the reason why my son was experiencing this.) Whatever the reason, I wanted it to stop. I hated seeing the fear in my son's eyes. I decided to let him sleep in my room until I knew he was emotionally ready to sleep in his own room again. It took some time for him to adjust to his father not living with us, but eventually he did.

When I was a single, unmarried woman, I told myself that I did not want a marriage like my parents'. I wanted something better: a healthy relationship without secrets built on mutual respect and unconditional love, no longer "I" but "we." I wanted my children to grow up in an emotionally healthy household. There have been days when I've wondered if I would have married someone different if my father had affirmed me as a child into my adulthood. I was ultimately blinded by the way François expressed his love for me, which was something I craved because I did not get it from my father. This was why the nightmare ending to my fairytale beginning was so devastating.

Chapter 5
Letting Go

In January, the same month in which François and I met with the counselors, I started working part-time as a legal assistant. The first client with whom I worked was filing for divorce. I was already going through my own painful separation and I took on the client's pain as he shared it with the lawyer. I was so overwhelmed that I had to step out of the room to hide my tears. Out of all the cases I could have assisted, *why did the first one have to be a divorce?* At the time, I did not understand why God had me working there, but I would find out towards the end of the year. Though that first case amplified my pain over my marital situation, it also helped me acquire the skills I would need to finally let go and start to live again.

During François's and my separation, I did not set boundaries in my desperation to get my husband back, which allowed my heart to be broken again and more deeply than before. Although we were living in separate apartments, we had a couple of encounters that belonged in a committed marital relationship. For example, in May, François took me and our son on an all-inclusive trip to my birthplace, St. Maarten, for a week. (François had promised me this trip before our separation.) I assumed he was using this opportunity to get away from family and friends to try to fix our relationship.

Though some of my friends and family opposed the trip, I took a chance and went. At the very least, this trip would allow me to attempt to reconnect with François. My friend Gabrielle requested that I check in with her daily. She did not trust François, and both she and her husband felt that I should have declined the invitation to go on the trip. Even with what we were facing, I did not think that François would physically harm me. Still, I made sure that my family had all of our travel information, and I emailed Gabrielle several times to let her know that I was okay.

When we departed for St. Maarten, I thought we were working towards reconciling as husband and wife, but I could not have been more wrong. We were not on the same page. I had had faith that there was a chance for us to start afresh. I had been so caught up in the lies François told me and in the nice things he would do for me, such as continuing to financially support our son and me, that I did not realize I was being played. Instead of reconciliation, I found myself in the middle of a love triangle. There were clear signs that the other woman was still in his life. One involved seeing her profile photo and name on a messaging app on his phone while we were having a meal on our trip. As I glanced at his phone, it appeared as if she was one of the last people with whom he had communicated via the app. When I brought it to his attention at the table, he denied everything. The app just *happened* to be open to her profile.

Several months after that fateful trip, François made a statement that not only hurt me but also woke me up. He said that he wanted the best of both worlds—being a bachelor and having a wife. In some ways, I felt that it was my fault because I had allowed it. My fear of moving forward without him had caused me to settle for an unhealthy relationship. Due to my faith that we would eventually reconcile, I had chosen to have a part-time husband instead of a man who was fully committed to making our marriage work. It was one of the most painful and humiliating experiences I have gone through, though I finally realized that I deserved more. I was worth more than a man who only wanted me some of the time. Holding on to someone who had already moved on had done more damage than good. Lesson learned.

Throughout the remainder of our separation, I felt that François was flaunting his relationship with the other woman, although he never admitted to having an affair despite my proof to the contrary. He lied to both me and his family about the status of their relationship: she was either "just a friend" or a "jealous co-worker." What killed me the most was that they were spending time together with our son. How could he do this so comfortably? What message was he sending to our son—that it is okay to entertain a relationship with another woman while you are separated? Separation does not mean divorce. You are still married. To the secular world his behavior may have been okay, but on paper and in my and God's eyes, we were still married.

Separation was wreaking havoc on me emotionally and physically. For most of my life, I had struggled with migraines, but they had become more intense than ever before. On one occasion, I had to leave my job in the middle of the day to go to the emergency room. My vision was blurred. The whole left side of my body felt numb. I thought I was having a stroke. I remember leaving the office crying. I do not know if I was crying because of the migraines or because of what was happening in my personal life. Either way, I was overwhelmed. When I finally was seen by a doctor, he assured me that I was not having a stroke. He even made a joke about how I had probably searched my symptoms on the internet and self-diagnosed; that was neither appropriate nor helpful. My mother felt that it was the separation and the stress that came with it that had caused my symptoms. She yelled at me for letting it get the best of me. She reminded me that I had a son to take care of and that I could not let this situation cause me to have a stroke.

As the weeks went by, I was still having the same symptoms, so I finally went to see a neurologist on a Tuesday afternoon in late October. After my initial appointment, the neurologist ordered an MRI. Since I was paying out of pocket, his office referred me to a location that had a special of $300 for the procedure. At the time, François was providing both spousal and child support, but I did not have the money readily available. I decided to reach out to him, and he agreed to pay for the test and to give the money to me that Friday. My appointment was scheduled for the following Tuesday. Unfortunately, he did not come through and I had only three days to acquire the necessary funds. I panicked. Where was I going to find $300 in such a short time? I did not want to ask anyone for a loan because I was not sure how and when I would be able to pay them back. I did not know what to do. Canceling the appointment seemed to be the only solution.

The next day (Saturday) was a turning point for me. With less than 72 hours to go before my appointment, it was placed on my heart to sell my wedding ring sets. The first set consisted of my engagement ring and wedding band. The second set was an upgrade both my son and François had presented to me a few months before our fifth wedding anniversary when he asked me to marry him again. I called my friend Gabrielle and asked her if she knew where I could sell my rings. She did, so she and her husband picked me up in their car a short while later and drove me to the first location they had in mind.

True to form, Gabrielle kept asking me if I was sure I wanted to do this, while her husband focused on ensuring that I received as much as possible for my rings. He rejected the offer from the first vendor we visited, certain that I could get more elsewhere. He turned out to be correct when the second place at which we stopped made a better offer. It was then that I knew I was ready to move forward, to part ways with the rings, and to prepare to file for divorce. It was a bittersweet moment, but I knew what I had to do. On the car ride home, Gabrielle kept checking to see if I was okay. I assured her I was fine. I had the money to pay for the test plus some extra cash. I had the MRI done three days later. My results were normal and after submitting my migraine journal to my neurologist, I was diagnosed with chronic migraines.

Walking away from my marriage was one of the toughest life decisions I have ever had to make. I had known for months that I would have to be the one to file for divorce, but I could not decide when to do it. I felt François should have been the one to file because *he* was the one who no longer wanted to be married to *me*. I had to be sure that I wanted a divorce. I am not saying getting a divorce is always the answer. I hate divorce. God hates divorce. I have seen marriages become stronger after overcoming situations like mine. However, both spouses have to fight for a marriage to work. In my case, I was the only one fighting. This experience taught me that you cannot make someone choose you. You cannot make someone want you. You cannot make someone fight for you. François had made it more than clear that reconciling as husband and wife was not what he wanted. Towards the end of December, two months after I sold my wedding ring sets, I began preparing my paperwork to file for divorce.

> *This experience taught me that you cannot make someone choose you. You cannot make someone want you. You cannot make someone fight for you.*

I do not believe it was a coincidence that I was working as a legal assistant at the time. I did not need to pay someone for legal advice because I had learned so much at the law office. With both hands-on experience preparing documents for clients and the ability to follow the directions on the self-representation packet provided by the clerk's office, I was able to submit my paperwork the following month without a hitch. Once all of the requirements were met, the divorce hearing was scheduled for May. I did not expect things to move so quickly.

On the morning of my scheduled divorce hearing, I decided to take the bus instead of driving to the courthouse. Looking back, I am glad that I did because I do not think I would have made it home without having an emotional breakdown in my car. As I gathered my belongings to leave, my mother called to check up on me. She tried to convince me to take a ride from either her or my father, but I just wanted to be alone. My mom shared some words of encouragement and we said our goodbyes.

There I was, standing at the bus stop in all black, holding up my umbrella. When the bus arrived, I entered, paid my fare, and took a seat. I had brought a book to read, but when I opened it, I could not get through even one paragraph. I had too much on my mind. This was going to be a day that would change my life forever. I simply stared out the window for most of the bus ride.

When I arrived downtown, I became numb. As I walked to the courthouse, I felt hurt, angry, and ashamed. I was screaming on the inside. Nevertheless, after going through security and stepping off the elevator, I showed no emotion. I took a seat on the bench in the hallway along with the other plaintiffs. Even though I was among people who were there for the same reason, I still felt ashamed. I felt that

I had let down my son, my parents, and, most importantly, God. I had biblical grounds to go through with the divorce, but there was always a voice inside my head that told me, "You did not do enough. You did not pray enough. You did not fast enough." Yet there I sat, this young Christian woman about to have her divorce papers signed, sealed, and delivered by a judge who probably did not care about her story.

After checking our paperwork, the court officer called all of us into the courtroom.

Wait...what? We won't be called individually? I was already feeling ashamed and now strangers were going to know all of my business!

The process went by so fast. Inside the courtroom, each plaintiff was called individually to the counsel table where the judge asked a series of "yes" or "no" questions about the divorce complaint to confirm its accuracy. Once confirmed, she read the final judgment of divorce (divorce decree) aloud, then signed and sealed the document. The judge wished me the best and the officer handed me my divorce documents.

When I returned home, the first person I called was my mom. She gave me comforting words to help me start the healing process. I texted my siblings and close friends to let them know that the divorce was official. Some of them offered to come over, but I wanted to be alone. I needed time to process what had just taken place. I consider that day to have been one of the worst of my life.

Because I represented myself in the divorce, I was the one responsible for serving my ex-husband with any related documents. I even had to provide him with his copy of our final judgment of divorce to let him know that our union had been officially dissolved. Even though we were co-parenting, and I usually saw him when he dropped off our son from preschool or picked him up on weekends, he was the last person I wanted to see that week. I was so broken. The pettiness in me contemplated giving him the documents weeks later, but I decided to just wait a day or so before I handed him the documents in a sealed manila envelope.

Two days later, on a Saturday morning, my siblings, my son, and I were scheduled for a morning photo session with my photographer friend. Even with the hurt I was feeling on the inside, it felt good to do something fun with people I loved. Later that day, my sister and I attended a graduate school commencement ceremony for our friend from church, followed by a dinner party at a local restaurant to celebrate her brother's birthday and her commencement. That day was not about me. We were celebrating our dear friend's recent accomplishment. I did not allow my emotions to control me. Only a handful of people knew about what had taken place in my life just days prior, so it was easy for me to hide my pain with both makeup and the masked smile I wore that day. From that week on, though, I began the process of healing from François's betrayal(s) and my divorce, which would be far from easy.

Chapter 6

The Healing Process

My road to healing was a painful journey. It took longer than I expected, but God saw me through it every step of the way. Healing was a process, one that would have been much more difficult without the emotional support of my family and friends. One of the church leaders I met the day I went for counseling with François proved to be a Godsend who walked alongside me throughout the entire journey. At times I struggled to reach out to her because I did not want to burden her with what I was going through, but she assured me that that was not the case. During our phone conversations and in-person meetups, she allowed me to be myself and provided a safe space to vent. She prayed with me. She cried with me. I hated crying in front of others, but she showed me that it was okay to cry and to be vulnerable sometimes. The strength I saw in her gave me hope that I would be able to get through this.

I also had male friends who provided support on my road to healing. Some were like brothers to me, so I felt comfortable enough to have transparent conversations with them. It was good to get a male perspective on what I was facing. Though we were able to have candid conversations, my guard was up. At times, I questioned their motives for being a friend to me; I felt they must have wanted something from me. I had to stop thinking that they were out to hurt me like François had. They were just trying to help.

Four weeks after my divorce was finalized, I received an email from Staples containing a receipt for a purchase. At the time, my ex-husband and I still had both of our names on a Staples Rewards account, for which my email address was the main address. Since I had not made the order, I assumed he had made the purchase. I was used to receiving emails about the office supplies he purchased for his business, but this order was different. It was for two hundred "printed invitations" and postage stamps.

My heart sank. I didn't know if these were invitations to an engagement party or if they were "save the date" reminders for a wedding, but something deep inside told me that my ex-husband was moving full-speed ahead with the woman for whom he had left me. It was tempting to investigate further, but I refrained from looking into the matter. Weeks later, I found out through an acquaintance who had been invited to François's engagement party that my suspicions had been correct. I do not know why she told me. It was the last thing I wanted to hear. I was in shock. The news hurt me to the core. I was sick to my stomach. François was indeed making plans to marry the other woman. I could not believe he would do this. I was so hurt that I sent a text to my close friends about him that included cuss words. Those who are close to me know that even when I'm angry I do not cuss, so when they received the text, they knew something was very wrong.

Weeks later, François requested specific dress clothes be sent with our son when he picked him up for the weekend. I did not know for sure if it was for the party, but something told me it was. My hurt caused me to be petty towards François. I purposely gave him a hard time about the clothes, though I eventually gave them to him. A social media post by a guest at the party confirmed that I was right about that weekend. A photo from the engagement party was the first thing I saw on my news feed after I logged on to Facebook. It hurt me that some of the people who attended the event knew who this woman was. How do you celebrate the engagement of a couple whose relationship is founded on infidelity? One guest was honest enough to share with me how uncomfortable they had felt attending the event, arguing that they were trying to be supportive. Despite how I felt, I eventually had to let it go and not hold a grudge against such individuals. I felt like I was still trapped in a Lifetime movie, which made my journey to healing even harder.

François and his fiancée spent time as a family with our son; they went to Disney World and traveled to Canada for family events. I knew there was no way on God's green earth that I wanted to spend the next ten or more years co-parenting with them as a couple. No way! They did not share the same values, and I did not want my son growing up confused about the morals I was trying to instill in him. I refused to let that happen. This led me to pray to God as I never have before. On countless nights, I found myself on my knees banging on my bedroom floor, crying to God asking him to prevent this wedding. This woman had to go, and I refused to stop praying until she was out of my son's life.

For the next few months, I was in a very dark place. I wanted François dead. I wanted his fiancée dead. Every time there were reports of a tragic accident on the news I would wait and watch, hoping that I would hear their names listed as the victims. I wanted him to hurt. I wanted them to feel the pain I was feeling. Their relationship also caused me to behave out of character when I interacted with my ex-husband. Any time I saw them together when they dropped off my son, I became very cold. At drop-off, I had no interest in having a conversation with François. I did not even want to look at him, though I was always looking for a reason to get into a confrontation with him. It could have been something as minute as him not returning all the clothes I had sent with our son. I made nothing into something because I was bitter about their relationship.

In addition, I struggled with suicidal thoughts for a period. It was usually worst after I dropped off my son at preschool. I would contemplate driving my car into a tree. Even though I could (and would) not take my own life, those thoughts were intense. (There was a time I almost got into a car accident because I was so distracted by my thoughts.) Once I had returned home, I would sit in my car for nearly an hour weeping or in complete silence. I did not believe I had the strength to continue living. I thought about what would happen to my son if I were no longer here. Who would take care of him? In my darkest moments, I was reminded of God's love for me through reading the Bible and books of encouragement. I was reminded of what Jesus did on the cross for me. I could not give up on life. Even though the emotional pain seemed unbearable, I knew that God still had a purpose for my life. I had to hold on. My son needed me to live, and God wanted me to live.

My son means the world to me and letting him see me weep on my bad days broke my heart. One day I was sitting on the edge of my bed weeping when he opened the door to my bedroom and walked in. The minute he opened the door I remember wiping away my tears, trying to put a smile on my face. I tried to hide my pain, but he knew that something wasn't right. He asked me what was wrong and why was I crying. With tears rolling down my face, I told him that everything was fine and that I was okay. He placed his hands on my face and began crying with me. That made me cry even more. I embraced him while trying to keep it together. It was during moments like this that I knew I had to get better emotionally because I had to be strong for my son. I did this by reading parenting books and the Bible, journaling, and talking to fellow moms about what I was facing.

> *In my darkest moments, I was reminded of God's love for me through reading the Bible and books of encouragement. I was reminded of what Jesus did on the cross for me. I could not give up on life.*

There was something about being angry and hurt that allowed me to find superhuman strength to pack up my ex's belongings, which I wanted out of the apartment as soon as possible. I packed up ten boxes, along with a few large bags, of his things. For weeks, these boxes were stacked in my dining room, then the stairway, and, with the help of my brothers, finally made their way to the basement for storage until François picked them up. One of my friends jokingly suggested that I reenact a scene from the movie *Waiting to Exhale*, in which one of the characters sets her husband's belongings and car on fire in front of their marital home after he leaves her for another woman. My friend even suggested I get a wig in order to look more like the scorned woman in that scene. I never would have had the courage to do that on the front lawn, but the thought of it sure was funny. It was good to be surrounded by friends who could make me laugh in my time of pain.

During the early years of our marriage, I had started my own business coordinating weddings and other special events. I continued to do this while I went through a divorce. I have cried at pretty much every wedding I have attended, planned, or coordinated, but during this time the emotions were overwhelming. It was hard not to have a breakdown as the couples exchanged their wedding vows. All I could think about was my failed marriage. I felt that I was not enough for my ex-husband to keep his vows.

The healing process was a struggle. In addition to the unhealthy actions already mentioned, I did a lot of retail therapy. Whenever I had a free moment, I was either at the mall or online buying clothes for myself or my son. I did not buy expensive items and always made sure that whatever I purchased was on sale. (I never wanted to pay full price for anything, as it made me feel less guilty about my "therapy.") However, due to weight loss, I never even had the chance to wear some of the clothes I bought because they were too big! Other items did not look as good as I had once thought after sitting in my closet for so long. I remember looking at a dress I had purchased thinking, *Why did I even buy this ugly thing?*

In February, nine months after my divorce, one of my prayers was answered: François and his fiancée ended their engagement. I remember sitting in the car with my son in the parking lot of his doctor's office when I texted François to confirm whether he was going to take our son on Valentine's weekend and that's when he told me. That was the best news I had received in a long time. I sat in the car for a few minutes to collect myself because I thought this day would never come. I laughed and thanked God for answering my prayers. I smiled all the way home, but later I thought about how this breakup might have affected his ex-fiancée. Out of all the people in the world, I was thinking about her feelings and what she was probably going through. One minute I couldn't care less about her, the next I felt sorry for her. If he had been lying to me about their relationship, I can only imagine the lies he must have told her, too.

Four months later, François alerted me to a new relationship he was in. He told me he was bringing his girlfriend to our son's preschool graduation that June. François's news took me by surprise. One woman had just left my son's life and now another one had entered it. When the day arrived, I was not looking forward to meeting her. I thought François was moving too fast, but it was not my place or my business to say anything.

When it came time to introduce her to me at our son's graduation celebration, I could tell François was a little nervous. To make things easier on everyone including myself, I just went ahead and introduced myself, shook her hand, and walked away. Honestly, I did not want her there. It took me some time to accept her as the new woman in my son's life. I had to remind myself that she had not done anything to me. She was not the one who had hurt me. With time, I became cordial with her, which made it easier for me to accept her as my son's bonus mom.

In late August, God pressed it upon my heart to have a sit-down with François after attending the *Divorce and Remarriage* seminar at my church earlier in the year. During the seminar, the topic of asking your former spouse for forgiveness was discussed. At first, I thought that idea was crazy. *He* was the one who broke our marital vows. Nevertheless, during the seminar, I was reminded of the things I had done wrong in our marriage that required me to ask him for forgiveness. After I reached out to him, he agreed to meet with me after our son was dropped off at school on his first day of kindergarten.

In the days leading up to our in-person meeting, I cried almost every day. I am an emotional person and the thought of having to ask the person who broke *my* heart to forgive *me* took a lot of strength and courage. It also required tremendous humility. Replaying the painful memories in my mind was a lot for me to bear. On the Tuesday after Labor Day, my ex-husband and I finally had a mature conversation. We met at a local Panera Bread after we said goodbye to our son on his first day of school. We apologized to one another for the things that occurred during our marriage as well as after we were divorced. I never thought I would hear some of the words that came out of his mouth. He admitted that he had acted like a boy and not a man when he had hurt me in the past. It was a humbling experience. I am thankful that we are now both at a place where we are cordial so that we can co-parent our son as well as we possibly can. Though our conversation could not magically erase the pain of the past, it was yet another step on my journey to letting go and starting to live again.

Chapter 7

Rebirth

From the time I filed for divorce throughout the next five years, I was in a season of rebirth. I lost confidence in myself after my divorce. I often struggled with feeling that I was not good enough. Why else would my husband have chosen someone else over me? My involvement in the community played a major role in rebuilding my confidence. Serving in church ministry is something I have done faithfully ever since I was a child, but even during those dark times I believed that God had a purpose for me both in *and* out of the church. I have always been dedicated to using my gifts outside the four walls of the church. Serving in the community gave me an opportunity to do just that.

When I filed for divorce, I had recently joined the board of a nonprofit organization. Its mission was to provide affordable housing in my hometown of Montclair, New Jersey, both through the provision of lower-rent apartments owned by the organization and through assistance with home-buying. (I had actually walked past the nonprofit's headquarters a number of times in the past without knowing what it was!) Angela, a very supportive, older friend from church (we met when she joined the choir, of which I'd long been a part) brought me aboard; she thought that the organization would benefit both from my event-planning background and from my Millennial (i.e., younger) viewpoint.

One of my first projects was to help prepare a Super Bowl-related fundraiser we were hosting at a wine shop. Our star guest was an NFL player for the New York Giants, who would choose the winning raffle ticket for a set of tickets to an NFL game. I was in charge of the room layout, as well as ordering the food and the all-important wine. I was partnered with a fellow board member who was responsible for setting up the audiovisual aspect of the event so attendees could watch the football game. Before the event officially started, I found myself having a personal conversation with this man. To begin, he asked me about my marital status and whether I had children. *Why is this man asking me this?* As I politely answered his questions, I discovered that he also was divorced and had children. I shared a few things about what I was going through. He shared his experience with his divorce and what God had done for him during that season of his life. He assured me that I had nothing to worry about in moving forward, for God was in control and would provide for my needs. Though I'd heard those words before from family, friends, and church leaders, they had a different impact coming from someone who could understand the deepest pangs of my heart. Just when I thought I was only there to help behind the scenes for the event, God had something He wanted me to hear to encourage me to persevere. I walked away that night thinking, *I'm going to be okay, and I will get through this.*

It took me some time to be comfortable enough to be myself around my fellow board members. I came into the organization guarded. I was not looking to develop any friendships. When I initially joined the board, I was the only Millennial (someone born between 1981 and 1994). I felt unqualified and inadequate because I was not immensely knowledgeable about the problems the organization was created to solve. I was not confident about the gifts and talents I possessed. While attending my first board retreat, I looked around the conference room at the other board members thinking, *I do not belong here.* They were parents, homeowners, community leaders, advocates, and folks who were successful in their careers. Some of them were even old enough to be my parents.

Once I let go of my insecurities and began to see myself as God saw me, I was able to perceive that I did indeed have a place in this organization. Serving on the board stretched me tremendously, awakening dormant gifts I never knew I had. I coordinated the annual bowl-a-thon (an adults-only event involving tasty treats, a bar, and team bowling) despite knowing nothing about this type of fundraiser. I designed centerpieces using fresh flowers for a spring fundraiser with no formal floral design training. I even designed social media graphics and event collateral material! The more I trusted God, the more I stepped out of my comfort zone. The more I stepped out of my comfort zone, the more responsibilities I was given in the organization. The more responsibilities I was given, the more I grew as a leader. In those moments when I felt unqualified to take on a task or project, there was always someone within the organization who pushed me to do it because they believed in me. It is a blessing to have people push you towards greatness when you do not believe in yourself. From serving on committees to chairing committees to chairing one of the annual fundraisers, being a part of the organization was a transformational experience that boosted my confidence. I could indeed do anything I was asked to do through God who strengthened me.

Literally days after my divorce was finalized, Angela also introduced me (via email) to the leaders of an online forum in which women contributed to a blog where they shared stories, articles, and resources on faith, life, and community. The group was hoping to host a day-long retreat to bring their readers and contributors together to network and fellowship in person. (Somewhere along the way we decided to hold smaller quarterly events building up to the big day.) My

> *It is a blessing to have people push you towards greatness when you do not believe in yourself. . . I could indeed do anything I was asked to do through God who strengthened me.*

friend thought my event-planning skills were just what the organization needed to bring that vision to life. I was decidedly less sure than she was. Being introduced to this new group of women was slightly intimidating, but they welcomed me with open arms.

To kick off their new season, the founders hosted a luncheon for their blog contributors. On a beautiful summer afternoon, I had the pleasure of meeting this team of women. Though we came from different walks of life, what connected us was our love for God. Each person had the opportunity to introduce herself as we sat in a circle during the luncheon. Most, if not all, of the women were married with children. When it was almost my turn to speak, I became emotionally overwhelmed. Sitting in this circle surrounded by these married women who seemed genuinely happy, while I had been divorced for less than two months, was hard. I found myself yet again comparing myself to others. I looked at where they were in life and where I was not. They had what I had just lost: a marriage. When it was my turn to speak, I introduced myself and shared that I was recently divorced while trying to keep myself from crying in front of them. I was in a vulnerable place, but the encouraging smiles of the women put my heart at ease for the rest of the luncheon. I had the opportunity to chat with a couple of the women individually after we broke out from the circle. It was a chance for me to share a little more about who I was and how I was doing emotionally. It warmed my heart to know that I was surrounded by women who genuinely cared about how I was doing.

About a year after I joined this team of women, I became a contributing writer for the blog. I knew absolutely nothing about writing for a blog, but with the guidance of one of the founders, I was able to tap into a gift I never knew I had. Writing my second blog post for the organization was a defining moment for me. It was one of the most courageous things I could have done at that time. As the deadline to submit the post approached, I felt God nudging me to share the story about the day my divorce was finalized. But I was afraid. I was afraid of what people were going to say about me after my divorce became public knowledge.

The deadline came and went and still I had written nothing. Yet, God continued to nudge me to write the post. One night, I had trouble sleeping. I was a bit frustrated because I had to wake up early to take my son to preschool. After tossing and turning in bed, something made me lie still and look up at my ceiling. It was in this stillness that I was able to write the blog post. I brought my laptop into my room and said a prayer asking God for guidance on what to write. Though tears began to pour down my face as I typed my story, I was at peace. I knew this was what God wanted me to do. After I finished and saved my post, I was able to fall asleep without any trouble.

My post was published on the blog twelve days later. After I shared it on my personal Facebook page, I must admit I did not want to check my account. Throughout the day I began to receive texts, emails, Facebook messages, and phone calls from friends, acquaintances, and church leaders. In a matter of days, God showed me that there was a purpose for sharing my story. He began to connect me with young women who were going through difficult seasons in their marriages. The more I shared my story, the more courageous I became.

I continued writing for the blog and had the honor of speaking at the forum's one-day women's retreat. When I was asked to speak at the event, I was hesitant to accept the invitation. I did not feel worthy enough to be a speaker. *What did I have to say to this group of women?* I did not think what I had to say would be impactful, but with the help of God, I was able to put together my speech and share my story with a group of about sixty women of all ages. My talk was called *Courage to Share Your Story*. Believe me, I needed all the courage I could get that day. You would think all the presentations I did in college would have prepared me for this moment, but they did not. This was not a business presentation; it was something deeply personal I had to share. I had butterflies in my stomach all morning leading up to my talk. I even left the event room for a bit to shake off my nerves.

Then it was time. I opened my talk by sharing the blogpost about what happened on the morning my divorce was finalized; the process of submitting the post to the editors; and the result of having the courage to share my story. I encouraged the women to be strong enough to be vulnerable and to be courageous enough to come forward to share their own stories.

Later in the day, participants were asked to apply what they had learned in previous sessions by sharing a *slice* of their stories in our *Slice Slam* session. I opened the *Slice Slam* by sharing how God had been my provider. Towards the end of my slice the unexpected happened: I cried! I could not believe I cried in front of these women. These were not tears of sadness, though, but of gratitude. Even with all the financial difficulties I had experienced, God had always provided for both me and my son. Reading aloud how faithful God had been reminded me of His love for me. I do not know where I would have been (much less where I would be now) if not for God's love.

God not only used me to help the organization further its mission but to help me become the woman I am today. I am a woman who is no

> *Even with all the financial difficulties I had experienced, God had always provided for both me and my son. Reading aloud how faithful God had been reminded me of His love for me.*

longer ashamed of her story. I am more confident in myself. I am stronger and wiser. This community of women became a support system for me. Working with them challenged me to do things outside of my comfort zone. Through the sharing of stories, I found hope in knowing that I was going to get through this difficult season in my life. It was comforting to know that I was not alone. One thing I appreciated most about these women was their transparency. They were not afraid to share their past experiences and their current struggles. They became my big sisters and mothers in the faith. They were the answer to my prayer to be surrounded by women of God who were open and unafraid to share their life experiences.

Left to my own devices, I probably would have spent the days leading up to and following my divorce alone in my apartment, seething with anger and pain. By serving in the community, however, I was forced to put my sorrow aside and to focus on others. I discovered gifts and talents I never knew I had. Most of all, I learned that God was still able to use me in my brokenness. The future might still be uncertain, but I knew that He would always be there beside me, comforting, loving, and providing for me.

Chapter 8

In Transition

Two years after my divorce, I was forced to make the difficult decision to move in with my family in April. (My sister had recently married and moved out of our parents' home, leaving room for me and my son.) It all happened so fast that I barely had time to pack up my belongings the way I wanted to. For years, I had lived in one unit and my parents in another of their multi-apartment house. Now I was behind on rent payments because François was no longer able to provide the spousal support he had promised me. It's not that I hadn't been trying to find a way to support myself and my son. For example, three months earlier I had applied for a dream job that my friends and I felt had been created just for me. It was in the county I lived in and the salary was more than I was asking for. I thought this was the breakthrough I had been waiting for. After my second interview for the position, I was sure it was mine. Instead, the organization ended up hiring from within. I was devastated. The position would have allowed me to continue to afford to rent the apartment at the discounted rate my parents were charging.

I began moving my stuff into their apartment on the first floor while my son was away in Georgia with his father during his spring break. This allowed me to get more things done without having to find something for him to do to keep him out from underfoot. I was unmotivated to move downstairs, but my father was determined to get me out of the second-floor apartment so he could prepare to put it up for rent. It is true what they say: you never know how much stuff you have until you move. I had nine years' worth of belongings and memories in that upstairs apartment. My father and brother moved out most of the large furniture. I felt my father pushed me out of the apartment without thinking about how it would emotionally affect me. The only thing that seemed to be on his mind was how fast he could get me out of the unit. I felt that he was being insensitive, but I also understood that as a homeowner he had to make the financial decision that was best for him and my mom.

The last place I wanted to be living was in the same apartment as my father. This was the man who I felt had ruined most of my childhood. Living on the same property, but in separate apartments, was what I was accustomed to. I enjoyed having my own space. I was able to control how often I interacted with him. Now I had no choice but to see him every single day. I value my peace. Perhaps it sounds harsh to say, but if you are someone who does or says things that will disturb my peace, you are not someone I want to be around if I do not have to be.

Once I was fully moved into my parents' apartment, I stayed in my room most, if not all, of the time. I did not want to talk to anyone. I was disappointed with my situation. I felt that I had failed in life and that I had failed my son.

Even encouragement from my close friends was not enough to lift my spirits. I did not understand why God would put me and my son in an environment that could be emotionally unhealthy. I knew I should have been grateful to have a roof over our heads, but all I could think was, *How am I going to emotionally deal with my father after all he put me through as a child?*

When my son returned home from his trip with his father, he was devastated when he found out that we were now living with my family. It broke my heart to see my son cry the way he did. He no longer had his own bedroom. He now had to share a room with my brother. That was an interesting transition, especially since my brother was not used to sharing his room with a child. Instead of seeing clothes all over his room, he now had to get used to seeing toys on his floor. I felt hopeless – life did not seem to be working in my favor.

The Saturday after my son returned home was my birthday. I was not in the celebrating mood. I just wanted to stay home and be lazy all day. As the birthday texts were coming in throughout the morning, one text from a friend led to her treating my son and me to brunch at a local diner. I almost declined her offer because I was not in the mood to go anywhere that day. To my surprise, later that day my brother had pizza delivered for my son and me for lunch. Then, another dear friend delivered Cheesecake Factory to the house for our dinner. I was blessed by these kind gestures and knew that God had touched these folks' hearts to be a blessing to my son and me that day. Not only was my heart full of the love that was shown to me that day, but my stomach was also full as well. No one knew how tough my birthday week was, but that day reminded me of how blessed I was despite what I was facing.

Living with my family was not a smooth transition, especially for my son. He was already sad about our new living arrangements, but it made it particularly hard when he witnessed my father and me in a heated discussion. My son had never seen any man disrespect me or raise his voice at me, nor had he seen me in a less-than-civil discussion with anyone. After that, my son took on a new role as my protector. He would tell my father not to talk to me the way he did. He became a lion trying to protect what was his, his mother.

It broke my heart to see my son feel the need to stand up for me. I had to make him understand that we were having an adult conversation and that I was fine. Because of this, there was a lot of on-and-off tension between my father and me. This gave me the motivation to continue to look for full-time employment. My end goal was to get as far away as possible from this environment, so that I could raise my son in an emotionally healthy household.

Even though my goal was to move out sooner rather than later, I could not dismiss the fact that my father and son seemed to develop a special bond that year. My son enjoyed eating mangos or watermelon at the kitchen table with my father. During the summer, my son would go up and down the driveway on his scooter or bicycle while my father did yard work. My father would block the driveway with garbage cans to keep him from riding into the street. Any time my father went outside to do yard work, my son would always ask me if he could go outside, too.

Even so, I could not understand why God had me living with my parents. I began to ask God what I had done wrong to be in this situation. I felt I was under attack because my father always seemed to find a way to get into an argument with me, my mom, or my brother. One minute he was going above and beyond to help me get back on my feet, the next he was criticizing me for not doing enough to help myself. How do you uplift and put someone down in the same breath? He was pushing me further away from him than I already was. I wanted to tell him that he needed to make up his mind and to choose whether he was for me or against me.

On a late Saturday afternoon in August of that year, I had the honor of attending the 25th wedding anniversary of a couple who is dear to me. They renewed their vows in a beautiful outdoor ceremony under a gazebo at a local church. The wedding party consisted of young married couples which added a special element to this momentous occasion. As the couple passionately exchanged vows at the altar, there was no doubt that even after twenty-five years they were still madly in love with each other. After the ceremony, guests remained outside to enjoy a cocktail hour followed by a dinner reception inside the church hall. Once inside the church hall guests were seated at their assigned table. Moments afterward, the wedding party and couple made their entrance followed by the traditional wedding reception elements: the blessing of food, toasts, dancing, dinner, and cake.

One of the most moving moments of the evening was when their eldest daughter gave her maid of honor speech. As she stood in the middle of the dance floor facing her parents' sweetheart table, she talked about the love she saw throughout her parents' marriage. She talked about how her father set her standard on how her husband should treat her when she gets married. As I listened to her heartfelt speech, I tried to hold back my tears, but I could not. At that moment, I so desperately wished that I had had a healthy marriage as a model I could have followed. I wished that my father had shown me how a man was supposed to respect and love his wife. I wished that he had shown me how to never settle for less than God's best. I wished that I had a great relationship with my father (both as a child and now as an adult), but there was no denying that I did not.

Two months later, I attended a Women's Entrepreneurship Conference at my alma mater. During the conference, a young lady and her friend walked into the ballroom and sat at my table. As we began chatting, I found out that they were both Christians, which allowed me to put my guard down. Before the conference ended, we exchanged phone numbers to keep in contact after the event. I met with one of the young ladies, Alexis, five weeks later at my local Panera Bread. While we were there, we shared our experiences with our fathers. I barely knew Alexis, but I found myself having a deep conversation with her. She shared her testimony of how God had healed the relationship between her and her father. She believed that God could do the same for me. That was when I realized that I was only praying for a breakthrough so that my son and I could have our own place. I was not praying for my father's heart. After having that conversation with Alexis, I knew I had to change my prayers.

What also made the transition to living with my father hard was that sometimes his voice would trigger fear or painful childhood memories. Whether he was having a heated discussion with me or someone else, it took me back to the scared little girl I had once been. I hated that feeling, especially because it caused my heart to race. I saw this as a spiritual attack. When that happened, I found myself praying silently in my heart for God's peace to fill the place, reminding myself that I had nothing to fear. It was those silent prayers that helped bring peace to the atmosphere of our often-troubled home.

Not only did I have to cope with the transition of moving in with my family, but I also had to junk the car François had purchased for me the year before. It kept having mechanical issues. After four visits to four different auto shops and thousands of dollars spent, no one could fix the problem. Having no car for the next three years would be challenging, especially since I had responsibilities as a mom, employee, and community and ministry volunteer. I missed out on quite a few opportunities to support friends' events with their new endeavors.

I struggled with asking for help because I did not want to be a burden to anyone. Also, I had been in situations where people would hold over my head what they had done for me and I did not want to be in that position again. I had to let go of my pride and ask for help from my family and friends. Having my family adjust their schedules to make sure I had a car to get to work or handle my motherly duties was a blessing. Despite our differences, I am grateful to have my family. They have sacrificed so much for me and my son. I do not know if I can ever repay them for all that they have done for us.

Getting back on my feet was challenging. Regarding my event planning business, partnerships with local venues kept falling through. In my eyes, these had seemed like the perfect opportunities to build my brand, but each was short-lived. Going to countless job interviews with both local and major companies and organizations was staring to take a toll on me. During the summer, after moving in with my parents, I applied for so many jobs. To be considered as a candidate for some of the positions I interviewed for was a boost to my self-esteem. I was shocked to even get a call back from a few of them. There was one position I interviewed for, with one of the largest special-interest publishing companies in America, that was one of those dream jobs that would allow me to commute via public transit to New York City and would require me to travel both domestically and internationally. When I was not offered this position, as well as other opportunities throughout the year, it began to eat away at my confidence.

When I decided to explore career opportunities that I did not necessarily want, I found myself working in the very industry I wanted to walk away from – bridal! Out of all the places I could have been hired, it was a leading bridal retailer who hired me as a part-time stylist. I accepted the position with hopes that I would secure full-time employment elsewhere in the months to come. I had never worked in bridal retail before, so this position required me to step out of my comfort zone yet again. I found myself asking for help more than I was used to. Any opportunity I had to share God's light with an individual or a group brought so much joy to me. Working for the retailer showed me it's not always about what I can financially receive from a job. Do not get me wrong, the commission was nice when I got it. However, sometimes the even greater reward was how God used me to show His love for people.

I thought I was going to be working there only for a short period before finding a better opportunity, but then one year became two. When I was about to hit my third anniversary, I became disheartened. The pressure from management to meet our weekly sales goals was becoming stressful. Stylists were leaving the company for better opportunities, which left those of us who remained exhausted and overworked. Employee morale was low. I was not happy, but I continued to push through my disappointments with a smile on my face. There had to be more for me than this.

Every year in January my church invites the congregation to participate in a twenty-one-day fast. Participating in the fast requires a commitment to spending an extended time in prayer while following a specific diet. My church does the Daniel Fast, fashioned after the lifestyle of the Old Testament hero and author of the same name. The fast itself prohibits sugar, meats, and processed foods, allowing for meals consisting only of vegetables, fruits, and whole grains. At first, I was not motivated to join in because of the disappointment of not having a new job and car, which in my mind was what I needed to move towards being self-sufficient. I eventually decided to participate in the fast because I felt I had no choice but to trust God. I had nothing to lose and so much to gain. As we entered the third week I wanted to stop fasting. I kept asking myself, *What's the point of doing this? Are any of my prayers ever going to be answered?* However, I managed to push through my doubt and participate for the entire twenty-one days. The more I focused on what prayers could still be answered rather than those that hadn't been, the more I was motivated to stay committed to the fast.

The Monday morning after the Daniel Fast ended, I walked into the kitchen to make breakfast. While sitting at the kitchen table eating his breakfast, my father said to me, "Start looking for a car." I was taken aback. "What?" I replied. "Start looking for a car. I'm going to help you get a car." At that moment, I believed this was the reason why I could not bring myself to allow my doubt to be greater than my faith during the Daniel Fast. If I had not fasted for the entire twenty-one days, I'm not sure if I would have received that blessing through my father.

After visiting multiple car dealerships with my father over the course of about ten days, I finally found a car within my budget. The down payment from my father was a little over six times the amount I had saved in the bank. The amount he gave me was more than what I was expecting to receive from him. I was elated. Once I was done with all the paperwork and got the keys to the car, my dad left me in the parking lot of the dealership and went home. As I got into the car to drive home, all I could say was, "Thank you, Lord." I finally had my own car to get around in. Now that I had my own means of transportation, I felt that a new job was on the way.

About a year after applying for multiple positions in the nonprofit sector, I was hired to work for a faith-based organization. When I initially interviewed, I was not selected for the job. About three months later, the organization contacted me to let me know that the position was open again. Look at God! This time around the waiting process to know if I would be offered the position took longer than I expected. I thought it would take a few weeks, but it ended up being a couple of months! I was a bit frustrated and decided to continue job hunting while I waited. I did not want to sit around idly. I was determined that this would be the year I would leave bridal retail and work in the nonprofit sector. I wanted a job that would provide the same type of fulfilment and satisfaction that volunteering in the community gave me. I applied and interviewed with another nonprofit for a position that seemed ideal because of the job responsibilities and salary. If I was offered both positions, I knew I would have a tough decision to make. I wanted to make sure I chose the best opportunity if presented with two options. Thankfully, the decision was easy for me to make when only one of the organizations gave me an offer. I was now able to put the administrative and fundraising skills I had acquired through volunteering with community organizations to good use as a member of the donor relations department of a grace-based nonprofit.

> *There is no limit to what He can and will do for those who trust in Him.*

God's timing was perfect because I started my new job a month before the COVID-19 pandemic caused my state to shut down. If I were still working in retail, I would probably be experiencing financial hardship and may well have lost my job. Better still, for the first few months of the pandemic, my new position allowed me to work both at the office and at home, which afforded me the opportunity to be with my son as he struggled to adjust to lockdown and virtual learning. I am thankful once again for God's provision. There is no limit to what He can and will do for those who trust in Him.

Chapter 9

Still I Smile

I t's taken me a few years to get to a place where I can honestly say that I am truly happy. Things have not been easy. My life is far from perfect, but I have never laughed and smiled as much as I do now. I'm happier than I have ever been. There are moments when I even ask myself, *Who is this woman?* Due to my fear of being rejected, hurt, betrayed, and judged, I kept my emotions bottled up inside for most of my life. I believed I always had to be strong and have it all together (or, at least, to give the appearance of such). I am *still* working on this. Yet, I've learned that life does not have to be perfect for me to be happy. Happiness is a choice, and it is what I will always choose.

For many years, I resented my mother. I did not understand how she could marry a man like my father. If she had not married him, then I would never have had to go through all the suffering he put me through. Then I realized that if she had not married him, I would not be here! When I first drafted this book, I finally decided to tell my mom about the extent of the trauma my father had caused me. She was shocked; she knew that he favored physical punishments and that he could be heavy-handed, but she never imagined that he would mercilessly beat his own child like he had done to me that fateful night. She admitted that she was young and naïve and wholly dependent upon her husband to provide for her and her children. As I looked in her eyes, I knew she was telling the truth. The anger I had harbored for so many years melted into compassion.

While I no longer hold any resentment against her, my mother still grieves for what her children suffered at the hands of their father. She actively prays for those of us who are not married, asking God to grant us loving and godly spouses who will treat us and any children we may have well. Even though my childhood was a painful and sometimes traumatic experience, I know now that there was purpose in my pain. Without these familial trials, I would not be the parent I am today, one who is determined to break the cycle of family dysfunction and abuse.

Through all the hurt and pain, God never left me. What I experienced during my separation and divorce could have left me angry and bitter, but God has since restored my broken heart. What I once viewed as a shattered dream can still be my reality. In His timing, I believe I will have my heart's desire of being married with more children. I now know the importance of having my priorities in order in marriage, family, and life – God, family, and everything else, in that order. I will continue to fight in prayer to break the cycle of generational family dysfunction. I also hope and pray that my relationship with my father will be restored sooner rather than later.

Holding on to the past used to keep me from experiencing the gift of joy. I have discovered that it is one of the greatest feelings in the world to let go of the past and forgive those who have hurt you. This was not something that happened overnight for me. The journey was long and difficult. I went from being married to being separated to being divorced and in a co-parenting relationship with my ex-husband. I was initially angry, hurt, and confused. I never imagined that I would be raising my son in a single-parent home. But God has kept us, provided for us, and healed me. Through prayer, counseling, and a whole lot of venting to the right people, I was able to get through one of the toughest seasons of my life and eventually feel freer than ever before.

God has blessed me with an amazingly talented son who has a smile that can light up a room. He has also blessed me and my son with a village of people who genuinely care for us, support us, and pray for us. They have kept me from losing my mind as I continue to navigate single motherhood. God has shown me the importance of community and family, and, perhaps most importantly, that I am not meant to go through this thing called life alone.

Co-parenting can be a lot of work when a child is being raised by parents whose lifestyles and values are sometimes at odds. Regardless, I know that I have a duty to raise my son to follow the Lord. Though François and I are not always on the same page, one thing on which we do agree is that we want our son to flourish in life. If our son loses privileges in one household, we try to make sure the same goes in the other. Open communication has been key to having a drama-free co-parenting relationship. We do not always get it right, especially when our texts to each other end up being misunderstood. (I have learned the hard way that some conversations are best had via phone rather than text.) As our son grows older, it is my prayer that even with the different lifestyles of his parents, he will become a God-fearing man of integrity and good character.

Being a single mom has been both rewarding and challenging. There have been days when I told God that I do not know if I was cut out for motherhood. When faced with challenges as a mother, I would sometimes feel defeated because things were not going the way I expected them to. I would play the blame game, blaming myself for some of the challenges I have faced with my son. I'm

> *While embracing my season of singleness, I have recognized how important it is to not rush into a relationship out of the fear of being lonely.*

still learning not to compare myself to other mothers. I try to remember that parents face many of the same challenges in childrearing regardless of whether they are married, and that God is both with and for me in all aspects of life, including parenthood.

While embracing my season of singleness, I have recognized how important it is to not rush into a relationship out of the fear of being lonely. Even before my divorce was final, I had friends who tried to convince me to begin dating. This was completely against what I stood for because I was still married. Once my divorce was finalized, I wanted to focus on true healing rather than just than fill the emptiness with a man. I wanted to make sure that I was emotionally healthy before I even began to consider dating. I also knew that I was not ready to trust just anyone with my heart.

Nevertheless, the pressure to date is real! Most of my friends are married, so any time I'm with them, my dating life (or lack thereof) seems to be a big topic of discussion. I believe they mean well, but it can be a bit much. At times they make me feel that I am not complete or that something is wrong with me because I do not have a boyfriend or husband. Due to what I experienced in my former marriage and what I have witnessed in my parents' marriage, I want to wait on God's timing. Even then, I must be careful about who I choose to date and spend the rest of my life with. Also, as a mother, I want to be even more careful about who I choose to bring into my son's life. I want God's best for both me and my son. This season of life has taught me to never allow anyone to pressure me into dating to meet their expectations of where I should be in life. I am thankful for like-minded singles who remind me to embrace this journey with grace.

Just when I thought I was doing an okay job of letting people in, my girlfriends made it clear to me that I am still standoffish, protective, and have my guard up, something men can sense. Gabrielle, of course, is constantly in my ear about the vibe I give off to men: "Do not say anything to me, just keep walking." Once I was no longer lost in my feelings and had time to reflect, I realized that I had been pushing people (especially men) away without ever giving myself the opportunity to get to know them or vice versa.

One of my biggest fears is having my heart broken again. I need to remember that not every man is like my father or François. I would like to be able to develop friendships with my brothers in Christ, not only because God has called us to live in community, but also to learn what a man who genuinely loves and walks with Christ looks like and how a woman should expect to be treated by the men in her life. And who knows? Perhaps one of these future friends will be the one I have been waiting for!

With each new day, I believe I am closer to receiving everything I have been praying for. I believe everything I have experienced in my life thus far is preparing me for those things. In my season of waiting, it is sometimes difficult to remain encouraged especially when I see others receive the blessings my heart desires. In the beginning, I felt entitled to receive those blessings. This thinking was short-lived after hearing a sermon during which I felt like I was the only one in the room to whom the pastor was speaking. The pastor spoke about how easily you can feel animosity towards someone who receives a blessing you were praying for before you do. While you were faithfully serving and living right in the eyes of God, that person was living his or her best life without even thinking about God. I felt convicted because I was a faithful servant who felt that way. I had to do a heart check and change the way I looked at my situation. I have much to be thankful for, and I must focus on those things.

God has been with me through it all, even when I was too bereft or depressed to feel His presence. His timing has always been the best for me. I do not need to worry about the future because God is with me and He is for me. God is working all things for my good.

Consequently, despite everything I have been through, I still have a reason to smile.